Wait

A WALK THROUGH THE PSALMS

PSALMS 31-60

by

KRISTIN SCHMUCKER

Study Suggestions

Thank you for choosing this study to help you dig into God's Word. We are so passionate about women getting into Scripture, and we are praying that this study will be a tool to help you do that. Here are a few tips to help you get the most from this study:

• Before you begin, take time to look into the context of the book. Find out who wrote it and learn about the cultural climate it was written in, as well as where it fits on the biblical timeline. Then take time to read through the entire book of the Bible we are studying if you are able. This will help you to get the big picture of the book and will aid in comprehension, inter pretation, and application.

• Start your study time with prayer. Ask God to help you understand what you are reading and allow it to transform you (Psalm 119:18).

• Look into the context of the book as well as the specific passage.

• Before reading what is written in the study, read the assigned passage! Repetitive reading is one of the best ways to study God's Word. Read it several times, if you are able, before going on to the study. Read in several translations if you find it helpful.

• As you read the text, mark down observations and questions. Write down things that stand out to you, things that you notice, or things that you don't understand. Look up important words in a dictionary or interlinear Bible.

• Look for things like verbs, commands, and references to God. Notice key terms and themes throughout the passage.

• After you have worked through the text, read what is written in the study. Take time to look up any cross-references mentioned as you study.

• Then work through the questions provided in the book. Read and answer them prayerfully.

• Paraphrase or summarize the passage, or even just one verse from the passage. Putting it into your own words helps you to slow down and think through every word.

• Focus your heart on the character of God that you have seen in this passage. What do you learn about God from the passage you have studied? Adore Him and praise Him for who He is.

• Think and pray through application and how this passage should change you. Get specific with yourself. Resist the urge to apply the passage to others. Do you have sin to confess? How should this passage impact your attitude toward people or circumstances? Does the passage command you to do something? Do you need to trust Him for something in your life? How does the truth of the gospel impact your everyday life?

We recommend you have a Bible, pen, highlighters, and journal as you work through this study. We recommend that ball point pens instead of gel pens be used in the study book to prevent smearing. Here are several other optional resources that you may find helpful as you study:

• www.blueletterbible.org This free website is a great resource for digging deeper. You can find translation comparison, an interlinear option to look at words in the original languages, Bible dictionaries, and even commentary.

• A Dictionary. If looking up words in the Hebrew and Greek feels intimidating, look up words in English. Often times we assume we know the meaning of a word, but looking it up and seeing its definition can help us understand a passage better.

• A double spaced copy of the text. You can use a website like www.biblegateway.com to copy the text of a passage and print out a double spaced copy to be able to mark on easily. Circle, underline, highlight, draw arrows, and mark in any way you would like to help you dig deeper and work through a passage.

Yet I Will Trust You

WEEK ONE · DAY ONE

What do we do when life seems impossible? What do we do when it seems that we have been forgotten in our waiting? It is at these times and at every other time that we must run to the Lord. We run to Him because there is no other place for us to run. There is no other shelter or refuge for our souls. We find David pleading the character of God, and we can do the same as we pray. We cry out, "You are righteous, be righteous in my situation." We ask Him to be who He is. In verse 2, David asks God to be a rock of refuge, and then in verse 3, he declares that God is just that. We should do the same, and pray God's Word and His character back to Him. This should serve to remind us of the necessity of being in the Word because we cannot call upon His character in our distress if we do not know His Word. We can come to Him claiming His character and find confidence in who He is. We are pointed to Jesus as we see the words that Jesus spoke from the cross, and we are reminded that we can pray this every day. Because He has redeemed us, we can place everything in His hands.

In verse 7, in the midst of his troubles David says that he will rejoice. We can rejoice because of what God has done with confidence that He will do it again. David says, "You have known the distress of my soul." How often we feel like no one understands us—but our God knows. The Hebrew word here conveys a knowledge by experience. Jesus knows because He has experienced every emotion we face (Hebrews 4:15-16). David was honest, real, and transparent with God, and we can be as well. We don't have to hide our emotions from Him. We can lay every emotion and every situation at His feet. We can lay it down and say, "This is how I feel. Show me what is true." This whole psalm shows us David wrestling with truth and perceived truth. There is what is true, and then there is what we perceive to be true, or what we feel, and they do not always line up. So we must come to the Lord and ask Him to show us what is true—and He will. In verse 22, David let his emotions take over. He felt he had been forgotten, but we know that God was with him even in the moments that it didn't feel like it.

We must live based on truth, not on our feelings. The truth is that His goodness is more abundant than we could ever imagine (v.19). The truth is that He is sovereign in our lives (v.15) and that He works all things for our good (Romans 8:28). The truth is that He shows His love and faithfulness right in the middle of our circumstances (v.21). The truth is that He hears us (v.32). The truth is that we don't have to fight our own battles because He will preserve us (v.23). The truth is that we can wait on the Lord—and this waiting is really trusting. So we can look at our life, and then we can look at Him and say, "Yet I will trust You."

WRITE OUT AS MANY CHARACTER TRAITS OR ATTRIBUTES
OF GOD THAT YOU CAN THINK OF.

WHAT IS THE DIFFERENCE BETWEEN TRUTH AND PERCEIVED TRUTH?

WRITE OUT A PERSONAL PRAYER PRAYING GOD'S
CHARACTER IN YOUR OWN LIFE.

Surrounded by Grace

WEEK ONE · DAY TWO

Blessed are the forgiven. There is a sweet blessing in forgiveness, and this psalm speaks to that truth. This blessing isn't given to those who are perfect, but to those that are forgiven. This is hope for our sinful hearts. We find blessing in our sin being covered. This does not refer to us hiding our sin, but instead to God covering our sin in His grace. Our sin is covered by His blood and the atonement. This is the doctrine of propitiation, that our sin has been covered by His blood (Romans 3:21-26). This doctrine is seen in the Old Testament with Adam and Eve needing covering for their sin (Genesis 3:21), and with the picture of the Passover in Exodus 12:13. All of these pointed ahead to Jesus who would be the covering for our sin. In verse 5, David says that he was coming to the Lord acknowledging his iniquity and not covering his sin. We have no power on our own to cover our sin, but when we come to the Lord in confession, He promises to forgive us (1 John 1:9). The weight of the burden of our sin is released when we come to the Lord in confession and receive forgiveness.

If we confess, He will forgive. And if we are forgiven by Him, we can live in forgiveness. We can live free from the power of sin, and we can live free from the guilt that sin brings. May we never hold against ourselves or others what has been forgiven by God. After confession and forgiveness, the tone of the psalm changes. David declares that God is his hiding place and says that God preserves him from trouble and surrounds him with shouts of deliverance. Spurgeon points out that, "The gospel of substitution makes him to be our refuge who otherwise would be our judge." What a sweet truth that we are not only forgiven, but also brought near to God because of Jesus. We are surrounded by grace. He leads us with His eyes on us and will never let us go. Verse 10 declares that many are the sorrows of the wicked, but steadfast love surrounds the one who trusts the Lord. The righteous still have sorrows, but they also have His grace and His *hesed* love—that love that pursues and keeps covenant. The love that will not let us go, and this love makes all the difference.

Even in the midst of sorrow or suffering, we are surrounded by His covenant love. His sovereign hand is working even when we don't understand what He is doing. We can trust Him and be glad in Him as the end of the psalm reminds us. *Glad because we are forgiven. Glad because He is working. Glad because He is with us.* Because of who He is, we can be glad.

WHAT DOES VERSE 2 MEAN WHEN IT SAYS, "BLESSED IS THE ONE WHOSE SIN IS COVERED," AND HOW DOES THIS POINT TO JESUS?

REFERENCE ROMANS 3:21-26. WHAT DOES IT LOOK LIKE FOR US TO LIVE IN THE FREEDOM OF FORGIVENESS?

WHY SHOULD GLADNESS BE A MARK OF A BELIEVER?

*I Will Praise
You in the Waiting*

WEEK ONE · DAY THREE

This psalm is a lesson on praise. It begins with a command to shout for joy in the Lord. The joy of the believer is not based on circumstances, but on the character of God. We can have joy in Him no matter what life brings. In the same way, we can praise at all times because we aren't just praising for circumstances, but for His character. Verse 1 tells us that praise befits the upright. As the people of God, this is who we are. Believers should be known as people of joy and thankfulness, not as complainers. It is so easy to skip into a complaining spirit, but as children of God we must combat a spirit of criticism with a heart of gratitude and worship.

While the first three verses give us clear commands to worship, verse 4 begins telling us why we should praise. We praise Him for His Word. It is good, and it is how we know who He is. We praise Him for who He is and what He does. We praise Him for His glory revealed in His Word, His works, and His world. As the psalm goes on, we are reminded of His sovereignty over all, beginning in verse 8. We see that the earth obeys His voice, and we are reminded that we should as well. There is nothing that can stand against His plan. There is nothing that takes Him by surprise. His plan is from the beginning of time (Ephesians 1). We can take comfort in the truth that though things don't always go according to our plan, they always go according to His plan. How quick we are to try to live in our own strength. How quick we are to try to do it on our own. How often we forget to come to His Word or go to Him in prayer. How often our hearts run to worry. Yet He gently reminds us that our strength and salvation are from Him alone. If every army came against us, they would have no chance if God has declared us the victor. We can rest in Him. We can trust Him. We place our hope in His steadfast love that constantly pursues us. We trust Him with everything we are.

Let's not be women of half-hearted trust, but of total surrender. Trust Him with everything, even the things you tend to cling to. Give them to Him. And then praise Him. Praise Him in the waiting. Praise Him in the wandering. Praise Him in the times of joy. Praise Him in the darkest nights. Praise Him with confidence that He is good, that He will go with you, and that His plan for you will never fail.

WHAT CAN YOU PRAISE GOD FOR TODAY?

WHAT DO YOU NEED TO SURRENDER TO HIM?

WHAT DOES IT LOOK LIKE TO LIVE A LIFE THAT IS HOPING, WAITING, AND TRUSTING IN HIM?

Taste and See that the Lord is Good

WEEK ONE · DAY FOUR

This psalm gives us confidence in the Lord no matter what life brings. It is a promise that in every season and in every situation, He will be faithful to His people. Throughout the psalm we will see many superlatives; words such as "all," "always," and "never" will remind us that these truths are firm and secure. The psalm opens with a declaration by David that he will bless the Lord at all times and praise Him continually. David is saying that he will praise God no matter what. David also recognizes that we praise Him, or "boast" in the Lord, not because of any good in us, but because He is good. We must begin to see our identity in Christ and His impact on all things. When we praise God in every situation, we begin to see God in every situation. We don't just see Him in the good, we see Him in it all and trust that He is working in ways that we cannot see.

In this psalm, we will also see many references to the psalmist seeking the Lord. We can seek Him only because He sought us first (1 John 4:19). And we can have full confidence that when we seek Him, we will find Him (Jeremiah 29:13). Verse 5 tells us that those who see Him or look to Him are radiant. When we get just a glimpse of His glory, it will shine through us, just as it did for Moses who saw just a small bit of God's glory (Exodus 34:6-7, 29-35). Our lives should be a reflection of His glory. He has shone His glory in our hearts (2 Corinthians 4:6), and now we can reflect it to those around us. We look to Him by looking to His Word. His Word reveals Him, and it is on the pages of Scripture that we see His glory. Jesus Himself is with us on every side. He will deliver us. Verse 8 tells us to taste and see that He is good. Taste is an experience and something that is personal. We must experience Him for ourselves. We must behold Him. We must see who He is, and He is good. We are promised that those of us that seek the Lord will lack no good thing. *He* is what we need. This may not look like prosperity by the world's standards. We aren't promised material things; we are promised things that truly have value. *We get Jesus. He is the gift.* If all we had was Jesus, He would be enough.

Because we have Him, we can turn from evil, and do good, and seek and pursue peace. This is *shalom* peace. It is completeness, wholeness, covenant relationship, and peace with God. This is what we have because of Him (Philippians 4:7, Psalm 29:11, Isaiah 26:3). We seek Him alone. We pursue, chase after, or hunt this peace. We want Jesus. He is the One who is with us. He is the One who hears and delivers. He always hears and always answers, though not always in the way that we would expect. And even in suffering, He is near. This is not a wish; it is a fact. He is near to the brokenhearted. So often it is in suffering or weakness that we feel His presence most clearly. It is when we are so aware of our weakness that we can so clearly see His strength. We will face many trials or afflictions, but He will be there every step of the way. Verse 20 is a beautiful prophecy of Jesus—not one bone was broken. Though He was pierced and bruised for us (Isaiah 53), He was not broken. As His church, we are His body. This life may bruise us, but it will not break the people of God. We may be afflicted, but we will not be crushed by this life. Life may perplex us, but we need not despair. This world may persecute us, but our God will not forsake us. We may be wounded, but we will not be broken (2 Corinthians 4:8). Our God always redeems anything. He can bring good from whatever we face. *Seek Jesus. Pursue Jesus. He will never leave you alone.*

READ 2 CORINTHIANS 3:18 AND PARAPHRASE IT BELOW.

HOW DO WE SEE GOD'S GLORY THROUGH HIS WORD?

WHAT DOES IT MEAN TO TASTE AND SEE THAT HE IS GOOD?

Remind Me that I Can Trust You

WEEK ONE • DAY FIVE

In this psalm, David runs to the Lord in the midst of suffering. He pleads with God to fight for him. As we read these words, we are reminded that we can come in boldness and confidence as well. We can plead with God to come to our aid. We can be honest before the Lord and pour our hearts out to Him. Our God is literally standing between us and our enemy. He is our warrior who is fighting our battles for us. This life is spiritual warfare, and though people may be against us, Ephesians 6:12 reminds us that our enemy is not people, but evil and the evil one. Even in the midst of the battle of this life, we can have confidence that our God is with us. Spurgeon said, "The accuser of the brethren shall be met with the Advocate of the Saints." What a comfort to know that our God is on our side. And if He is for us, nothing can be against us (Romans 8:31).

The end of verse 3 is David asking God to remind him of God's goodness, and how often we need those reminders as well! His voice stills our anxious soul. David was in great trial, likely running for his life from Saul in this passage, and yet still his reaction was to run to the Lord. May the same be true of us. May our response to this life be to run to Jesus. When trials come, do I complain about it or pray about it? Do I take it into my own hands, or do I take it to the One who has power to change it? Philippians 4:6 reminds us that we do not have to be anxious about anything. Instead, we can come to the Lord in prayer and supplication, begging Him to work on our behalf, and then we can come with thanksgiving because we know that He will answer—and this leads us to rejoice in Him. Verse 10 says, "All my bones shall say, O Lord who is like you?" So despite everything that is happening around me, everything I am will praise Him. There is nothing and no one that can compare to Him. This world has nothing to offer that is better than Jesus. This is how David was treated, and this is how Jesus was treated, so we should not be surprised by opposition (1 Peter 2:19-24). Following Jesus often has a high cost, but it is always worth it.

Verse 22 reminds us that the Lord is not surprised by our situation, and His eye is always upon His children (Psalm 34:15). We cry out to Him to not be silent and to be near. We pray, "Lord, I can face anything if you are near." We cry for Him to vindicate. We don't need to slander others to prove ourselves right. We can lay it down for God to take care of. When we lay our burdens down at His feet it releases their power over us. And then we remind ourselves that it is for His glory, and not our own. We praise Him right in the middle of what we are facing with confidence that He is near and He will be faithful.

SUMMARIZE WHAT DAVID WAS PRAYING IN THIS PSALM.

HOW DOES IT CHANGE OUR PERSPECTIVE WHEN WE
REMEMBER THAT OUR ENEMY IS NOT PEOPLE?

READ EPHESIANS 6:12 FOR REFERENCE.
HOW DOES GOD CALM OUR ANXIOUS SOUL?

BE STRONG,
AND LET YOUR HEART
BE COURAGEOUS,
ALL YOU WHO PUT YOUR
HOPE IN THE LORD!

Psalm 31:24

WEEK ONE

Weekly Reflection ————————————————————

Read Psalm 31-35

PARAPHRASE THE PASSAGE FROM THIS WEEK.

WHAT DID YOU OBSERVE FROM THIS WEEK'S TEXT ABOUT GOD AND HIS CHARACTER?

WHAT DOES THE PASSAGE TEACH ABOUT THE CONDITION OF MANKIND AND ABOUT YOURSELF?

HOW DOES THIS PASSAGE POINT TO THE GOSPEL?

HOW SHOULD YOU RESPOND TO THIS PASSAGE?
WHAT IS THE PERSONAL APPLICATION?

WHAT SPECIFIC ACTION STEPS CAN YOU TAKE
THIS WEEK TO APPLY THE PASSAGE?

I Will Take Refuge in
the Shadow of Your Wings

WEEK TWO · DAY ONE

In this psalm, we will find a contrast. We first see the state of the wicked, but it serves to point us to the overwhelming beauty of our God. The wicked live with no fear of God. They live with an attitude of apathy toward the Lord. They live as if God doesn't matter. The wicked flatter themselves by thinking that they do not need God. May this never be true of us! May we never fool ourselves into thinking we can do this life on our own or that our sin isn't that bad. Instead, may we allow our weakness to point us to the Lord so that as we realize we can't do it on our own, we can run to Him for strength.

Our God's love and character are too wonderful for us to even comprehend. Yet we will spend our whole lives studying His Word to get sweet little glimpses of who He is. Verse 5 begins this beautiful section pointing us to the character of our God. Over and over we see the phrase "steadfast love," sometimes translated as "mercy" or "lovingkindness." This is the Hebrew word *hesed*, and it is so rich that it is difficult to translate into just one English word. We cannot help but be overwhelmed and in awe of this description of the Lord. There is nowhere we can go outside of His steadfast love. His love is relentless and pursuing, and everywhere we look it is there. His love is high above all—it is like a cloud that shields us. He is firm and secure, and unmovable like the strongest mountain. He is vast and unsearchable, like the depths of the sea. From the highness of heaven to the depths of the sea, His love is for us. His love and character compel us to worship. He is a feast for our souls and water for our thirsty hearts. He is the Living Water, and He is the Bread of Life (John 4, 6:35). He is abundant and more than enough for us. He is the Creator and Sustainer of life. We cannot see the light of spiritual things without Him. We see the light because He is Light (John 8:12), and by His grace, He makes us light as well (Matthew 5:14-16).

This passage is full of the beauty of our God. Tucked in verse 7, we find that we take refuge in the shadow of His wings. This concept is seen in many places in Scripture. It gives us an image of a bird shielding her young. Truly, He is our shelter from the storm and from the enemy. Nothing can hurt us when we are sheltered by His wings. This phrase also calls to our memory the ark of the covenant and the wings of the cherubim over the mercy seat. We have refuge in God because of His mercy at the cross. He took all of our punishment for us, and we are shielded under His wings of grace. The wings of a bird are often stained with her own blood as she protects her young from the enemies. The wings of our Savior are stained with His own blood that has been poured out for us. The cross stands outstretched for us like the wings of God's mercy. We find refuge in the cross where His outstretched arms and His precious blood cover us and wash us clean.

Our God calls us to come and find our rest in Him. As we see who He is, we are compelled to worship. We worship Him for everything He is, and we rest in the shadow of His mercy and grace.

WHAT DOES GOD'S STEADFAST LOVE TELL US ABOUT WHO HE IS?

WHY DO WE FIND COMFORT IN THE SHADOW OF HIS WINGS?

HOW DOES WHO GOD IS COMPEL US TO WORSHIP?

You Give Me the Desires of My Heart

WEEK TWO · DAY TWO

We could sit on this psalm for a week and not exhaust the depths of God's character revealed here. This psalm reminds us that God will never forsake His people, and it answers the age-old question of why "bad things" happen to "good people," and why "good things" happen to "bad people." The psalm begins with a command to "fret not," and we will see that this psalm is full of commands to the believer. "Fret not" here gives us the idea of kindling a fire. It reminds us not to kindle a fire of bitterness in our hearts toward others. They will fade and wither. They are not evergreen and always growing like the blessed man of Psalm 1. God is reminding us to look at things from His perspective. He can see the eternal side. He asks us if we will trust Him even when it doesn't make sense. He asks if we will trust that even what we don't have is because it is good for us.

The commands to believers continue in verse 3. We are told to trust Him, to do good, to dwell in the land and befriend or cultivate faithfulness. We are told to delight in the Lord. Not in our circumstances or our possessions, but in Him, and then He will give us the desires of our heart. This isn't a genie in a bottle—this is about heart transformation. As we become like Him, our desires become His desires. This is transformation. We don't need to rush ahead with our own desires. We can be still and rest in Him. We can wait on the Lord and trust His plan. We are assured of God's faithfulness to His people and of His justice against unfaithfulness. In this psalm we also see many references to the land, dwelling, heritage, and inheritance. Those were huge themes for the nation of Israel, but they are for us as well. For most of Israel during this time, this inheritance was promised land. This land was part of the covenant. But one tribe of Israel, the Levites, did not receive an inheritance of land. Their inheritance was God Himself (Deuteronomy 18:1-2). We are now under the new covenant, and our inheritance as believers is God as well. Ephesians 1:11-14 tells us that in Him, Jesus, we have obtained an inheritance! Not only that, but the Spirit has been given to us as a down payment of that inheritance. He is our inheritance.

Because of Jesus, we can have abundance in the days of famine (v.19). Because of Jesus, we can be confident that He is with us (v.24). Because of Jesus, we follow Him and abide with Him (v.27). Because of Jesus, we can cling to God's promises that find their yes and amen in Him (v.31, 2 Corinthians 1:20). Because of Jesus, we can trust Him, and wait for Him, and serve Him in the waiting (v.34). No matter what life looks like, we can place our confidence in Him and delight in the One who is our salvation. Spurgeon says of verse 39, "Sound doctrine this. The very marrow of the gospel of free grace. By salvation is meant deliverance of every kind, not only the salvation which finally lands us in glory, but all the minor rescues along the way, these are all ascribed unto the Lord, and to Him alone." Our God will not forsake His children. He alone is our refuge, and we will find our rest in His sovereign grace.

READ BACK THROUGH THE PSALM AND MARK ALL OF THE DIRECT COMMANDS TO THE READER.

HOW DOES GOD CHANGE OUR DESIRES TO LINE UP WITH HIS DESIRES?

THIS PSALM LISTS OUT THINGS THAT WE HAVE BECAUSE WE ARE BELIEVERS. TAKE A MOMENT TO WRITE DOWN SOME THINGS THAT CHRIST HAS DONE FOR YOU.

He is Our Salvation

WEEK TWO · DAY THREE

Psalm 38 is the third of the penitential psalms. The psalm begins with David inwardly focused on his sin and his condition. Then David focuses on his enemies. But when he shifts his gaze toward heaven, things change. When David focused on himself and those around him, he was discouraged, but when he shifted his focus to the Lord, he found hope. This psalm reminds us to focus on what we know and not just what we feel. When we feel that all is against us, we can be sure that God has not abandoned us. We may feel forgotten, but we never are. David's heart was heavy from the weight of his sin. In verse 4, he declares that his iniquity is too heavy of a burden to bear. Our sin is too heavy for us, but not for Him. The weight of our sin has been nailed to the cross and is overcome by the weight of His glory.

Conviction of our sin is not a bad thing. It leads us back to the Lord. Conviction should lead us to repentance and restoration, but when we ignore unconfessed sin, and dwell on it, we end up overcome and overwhelmed by guilt. Instead, we are called to turn from our sin in repentance and run into the arms of God. He knows every longing of our hearts (v.9). He is ready and waiting to restore. People let David down, even those closest to him, yet the Lord never had. You may feel lonely and abandoned by Him.

David sinned and messed up a lot, yet he kept returning to the Lord over and over again. God never changed once. He was waiting each time with open arms. At the end of the psalm, David returns to the Lord and finds hope for his heart. He came in confession and found grace. If your sin is too heavy—take it to Jesus. Lay it down at His feet. Come in your brokenness and let Him restore you. Spurgeon said, "When sickness, slander, and sin, all beset a saint, he requires the especial aid of heaven, and he shall have it too. He is afraid of nothing while God is with him, and God is with him evermore." What a comfort to know that He is with us evermore! The weight of sin points us to the beauty of redemption and the joy of restoration. There is mercy to be found at the cross.

HOW CAN YOU SHIFT YOUR GAZE OFF OF YOURSELF
AND OTHERS AND TO THE LORD?

HOW DOES CONVICTION LEAD US BACK TO THE LORD?

HOW DOES GOD'S WORD BRING HOPE TO US?

Live for What Matters

WEEK TWO · DAY FOUR

In this psalm, again we see David focused on himself at the start and on a desire not to sin. He specifically is seeking not to sin with His words. So with a desire not to sin, he chooses to be silent. Our words hold great power, and often result in more sin than our actions. So many passages of Scripture point us to the power of words and the great wisdom found in being careful with our words (James 3:5-12, Proverbs 10:19, 17:27-28,18:21). But as humans we desire to communicate, so the complete lack of speaking that David tried did not last long. In wisdom, he broke his silence to the Lord. When we feel words welling up inside of us that would not be wise to speak to others, we can turn to the Lord. He already knows the thoughts of our hearts. We can pour out our frustration and our longing to the One who has the power to change the situation and calm our soul. Ecclesiastes 3:1 tells us that there is a time to keep silent and a time to speak, and we must seek the Lord's wisdom to discern this. Wisdom with our words does not mean that we need to stuff our feelings; it means we can take them to the Lord and seek wisdom from Him. We need to ask God to change our hearts so that our words will then change.

David then focuses in on the shortness of life. It is like a breath or a shadow that quickly vanishes. And if life is short then we must live for what matters. We should focus on the things above and not just the things of this earth (Colossians 3:2). David points us to the truth that our hope isn't found in this world, but in God alone. Our hope is in Him. Our hope is not in this world, in popularity, position, or in financial security. Our hope is not in politics or in people—or even in ourselves. *Our hope is in Him*. David wrote this psalm near the end of his life as sickness began to take over, and yet he was able to call out to the Lord even then knowing that God shows up in our suffering. David calls himself a sojourner with God. He was not a stranger from God, but instead he was saying that this world is not our home. We are here temporarily, but we are living for eternity. Even here on earth, we can live for heaven. David was not alone in this earthly journey, and neither are we. C.S. Lewis said, "God whispers to us in our pleasures, speaks in our conscience, but shouts in our pain." Even when the night is long and we find ourselves in a difficult season—He is there.

READ JAMES 3:5-12, PROVERBS 10:19, 17:27-28, 18:21.
WHAT DO THESE TELL US ABOUT THE POWER OF WORDS?

WHAT DO YOU WANT GOD TO CHANGE YOUR HEART ABOUT,
SO THAT YOU WILL NOT SIN WITH YOUR WORDS?

HOW DOES THE TRUTH THAT OUR HOPE IS IN GOD'S
WORD CHANGE OUR PERSPECTIVE ON LIFE?

I Will Declare Your Faithfulness

WEEK TWO · DAY FIVE

This psalm of David is one thought to have been sung by the congregation. It relates to the life of David, but it is also a messianic psalm and is quoted of Jesus in Hebrews 10:5-9. There is a beautiful theme of God's faithfulness and how He has rescued His children. We wait for Him, and He has inclined or stretched out Himself to us. He has heard us and drawn us close to Himself though we were once far off (Ephesians 2:13). He took us from instability to the secure and solid rock of His character. He has given us a new song. We should sing the old songs of His past faithfulness, and also new songs of what He is doing right now. And as we praise Him for His faithfulness, it will cause others to trust Him as well. We are left in awe of who He is. Spurgeon said, "How sweet to be outdone, overcome, and overwhelmed by the astonishing grace of the Lord our God." We simply do not have enough words to tell of all that He has done for us. Our song must include our gratitude for the cross because this is the ultimate demonstration of God's faithfulness to us.

We are reminded that God isn't just looking for offerings and sacrifices. *Jesus was the plan from the beginning.* Offerings and sacrifices only point us to Him. God is not looking for religious people, but for hearts transformed by the gospel and surrendered to a relationship with Him. You see, this world won't always understand the message of who He is. But we can sing out no other message than who He is. David tells us to not hold back or restrain from preaching of His faithfulness and steadfast love, and then verse 11 tells us that God does not restrain His mercy from us. So we do not hold back telling of His faithfulness, and He does not hold back His mercy, but pours it out *freely*. His steadfast love, mercy, and faithfulness are what we cling to, because that is who He is. He is stronger than the chains of our sin. So when we don't know what to do, we must run to Him. In running to Him, we must praise Him for who He is. We will praise Him that He has delivered us, and that He is faithful, and merciful, and abounding in steadfast love.

READ THROUGH THE PSALM AGAIN. MAKE NOTE OF THE VERBS / ACTION WORDS. NOTE WHAT THINGS THE PSALMIST DID AND WHAT THINGS GOD DID.

HOW HAVE YOU SEEN GOD'S FAITHFULNESS IN THE PAST?

HOW DO YOU SEE GOD'S FAITHFULNESS TO YOU RIGHT NOW? LIST OUT SOME OF GOD'S ATTRIBUTES AND FOCUS ON WHO HE IS.

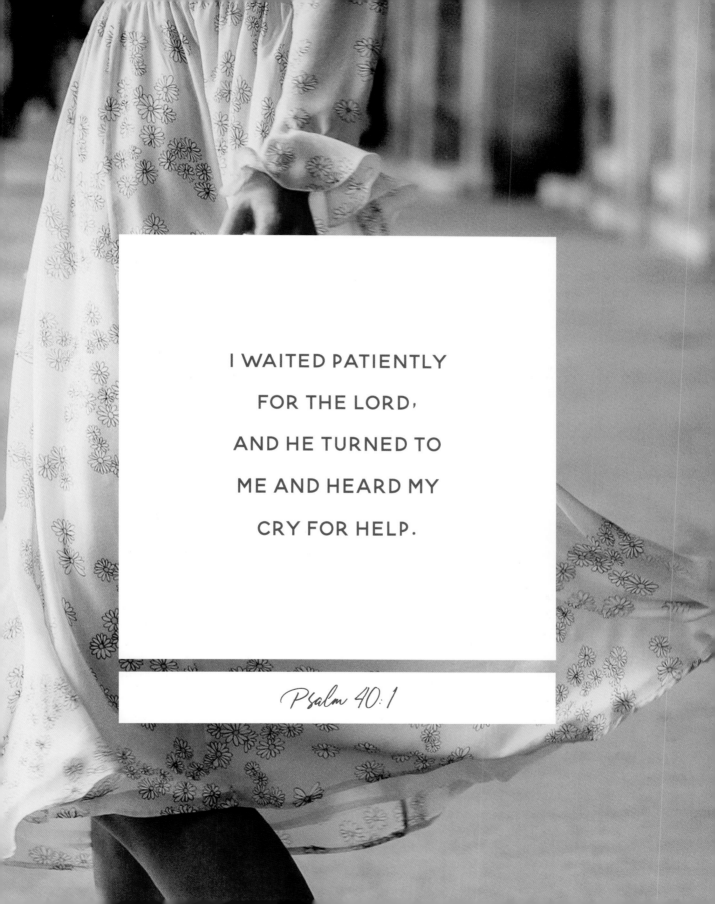

I WAITED PATIENTLY
FOR THE LORD,
AND HE TURNED TO
ME AND HEARD MY
CRY FOR HELP.

Psalm 40:1

WEEK TWO

Weekly Reflection ————————————————————

Read Psalm 36-40

WHAT DID YOU OBSERVE FROM THIS WEEK'S TEXT
ABOUT GOD AND HIS CHARACTER?

WHAT DOES THE PASSAGE TEACH ABOUT THE CONDITION OF MANKIND
AND ABOUT YOURSELF?

HOW DOES THIS PASSAGE POINT TO THE GOSPEL?

HOW SHOULD YOU RESPOND TO THIS PASSAGE?
WHAT IS THE PERSONAL APPLICATION?

WHAT SPECIFIC ACTION STEPS CAN YOU TAKE
THIS WEEK TO APPLY THE PASSAGE?

Blessed

WEEK THREE · DAY ONE

This psalm begins with a beatitude and takes our minds right back to Psalm 1. It tells us that the one who considers the poor is blessed. It also reminds us of the beautiful words of Jesus spoken in the Sermon on the Mount. This blessing is not prosperity or material blessing, but it is God's favor and His presence. This psalm serves to point us to Jesus who is our great example. We see David here as a type of Jesus, which means that his life serves to give us just a glimpse of the greater Son of David. In Matthew 5, Jesus tells us that the poor in spirit are blessed, and here we see blessing for those that care for the poor. Jesus is our example of caring for the outcast, the marginalized, and the broken. *Blessed are the ones who are like Jesus.* Jesus has poured grace out on us, and now we can pour grace out on ourselves and on others. The ones that follow Jesus are not immune from trouble or trial, but they are never alone in it. The Lord sustains and protects right in the middle of our struggles.

David comes humbly, pleading for grace and forgiveness, and giving no excuse for his sin. He comes assured and convinced of God's love for him, and this emboldens him to pray big and bold prayers. When we glimpse God's love for us, it enables us to pray with confidence, fully assured that He will do what is best for us. We don't have to fear praying the wrong thing. We can trust that He will work for our good and His glory. We see many references to Jesus and even words that Jesus would speak of Judas. In all that Jesus faced, there is nothing that could defeat Him. Even the grave had no hold on our Savior. And if even death has no power over Him, we can be sure that our problems are not too big for Him.

The psalm begins with saying "blessed is the one," and ends with "blessed be the Lord." The psalm points us to God who is the source of all blessing. It points us to the One who is eternal. His faithfulness has no end, and it is the dark nights that push us to His side and let His glory shine even brighter before us. Every promise is fulfilled in Jesus. He is the yes and amen (2 Corinthians 1:20). *From everlasting to everlasting. Amen and Amen.*

HOW IS GOD'S DEFINITION OF "BLESSED" DIFFERENT
THAN THE WORLD'S DEFINITION OF "BLESSED?"

WHAT DOES IT LOOK LIKE PRACTICALLY TO LIVE LIKE JESUS?

HOW DOES GOD'S LOVE EMBOLDEN US TO PRAY BIG AND BOLD PRAYERS?

My Soul Thirsts
For You

WEEK THREE · DAY TWO

Our hearts and souls should long, yearn, and thirst for our God. Psalm 42 is the first psalm in the second book of the Psalms, and this psalm typically attributed to David shows us the wrestling of David's heart. He thirsts for God. References to hunger and thirst are not uncommon in Scripture and are used in both the Old Testament and the New (Psalm 36:8-9, 63:1, Matthew 5:6, John 4:10-14, 7:37-39, Revelation 21:6, 22:17). Jesus Himself is the water of life, and this thirst is our coming to Him again and again asking for Him to fill us. We do not thirst for encouraging words or an easy life, but we thirst for God Himself. We find satisfaction in Him alone.

In verse 3, we can see that though David was thirsty for God, he was feeding on his own sorrows. He was in a season of suffering. We aren't exactly sure what he was facing, but his sorrow was great and even his enemies taunted him by asking him where his God was (v.3, 10). He looks back to better days spent in God's house and with God's people, but he found no comfort there. His soul was in turmoil inside of him. *Have you ever felt that way? Like there is turmoil inside of you?* David did what we can do as well—he preached the gospel to himself. He reminded himself of the truth instead of following his heart. We are so prone to follow the world when it tells us to follow our hearts, but Scripture tells us that our hearts are deceitful and wicked (Jeremiah 17:9). We don't need to follow our hearts—we need to follow God. David had to cling to truth and remind himself of who God is, and we must do the same when we are tempted to anxiety and despair.

In verse 8, David shifts to use God's personal and covenant name, Yahweh, as he praises God for the steadfast *hesed* love and sings a song of grace in the darkest night. Prayer and praise go together, and praise should always be a part of our prayer. David was honest with the Lord. He came and told God that he didn't understand. It wasn't that David was questioning God, but instead, he was asking God to show him from God's perspective. The psalm ends with a declaration of hope. The word "hope" here means "wait, trust, expect." We trust in Him, and we expect Him to work. We hope because of who He is. We wait and we trust with expectation. We know that He will be faithful because that is who He is.

WHAT IS THE EVIDENCE IN OUR LIFE THAT WE THIRST FOR GOD?

LOOK UP THE FOLLOWING CROSS-REFERENCES AND RECORD ANY OBSERVATIONS ABOUT HUNGERING AND THIRSTING FOR GOD. PSALM 36:8-9, 63:1, MATTHEW 5:6, JOHN 4:10-14, 7:37-39, REVELATION 21:6, 22:17

THIS WORLD TELLS US TO FOLLOW OUR HEARTS. WHY IS THIS BAD ADVICE?

Hope in God

WEEK THREE · DAY THREE

This psalm begins with a cry for vindication. The psalm contains some very similar themes and even direct quotes from Psalm 42, as we again see David in a time of trouble. David is asking God to fight for him and work on his behalf. We don't need to try to seek revenge when God is on our side. We can leave our problems and the people that wound us in His hands. We can have confidence in who He is. Our faith is more than wishful thinking; it is confident expectation. He is the place that we find our refuge, our hope, and our confidence. This world has no refuge to offer us, but God's arms are open to shield us from this world. David came to God with honesty and vulnerability. *God has not rejected us.* Our emotions may tell us this, but we can rest in the truth of His Word. He welcomes our questions, but if we could fully see His plan, we would not question. If we could see from His perspective, we would see that even our hardest moments were for our good (Romans 8:28). So we come to Him in prayer, and we pray for Him to help us see from His perspective, and most of all to help us trust Him even when our finite minds do not understand. David prays for God to show Himself and to lead. He pleads for God to lead and asks to dwell and commune with God even in the midst of the situation that he was facing.

The altar was the place where sins were washed away and fellowship was restored. It was a place of worship and renewal. *Jesus is the fulfillment of the altar.* He became the once for all sacrifice at Calvary so that we could come freely into God's presence and find fellowship with God, worshiping Him in freedom. This psalm reminds us that as God's people, the thing we truly desire is not just for our trials to disappear, but for us to fellowship and commune with God. *And it can happen right in the midst of our trials.* Like David writing the psalms in the midst of turmoil, like the three Hebrew children worshiping from the fiery furnace in the book of Daniel, and like the apostle Paul writing many of the epistles from a prison cell, we can have exceeding joy in the midst of the suffering and uncertainty that life brings because we have Him.

WHAT DOES IT MEAN THAT GOD IS OUR REFUGE? LOOK UP
A DICTIONARY DEFINITION OF THE WORD "REFUGE."

WHAT SITUATION IN YOUR LIFE RIGHT NOW CAN YOU ASK GOD
TO LET YOU SEE FROM HIS PERSPECTIVE?

HOW CAN WE FELLOWSHIP WITH GOD AND COMMUNE WITH HIM RIGHT
IN THE MIDST OF WHATEVER WE ARE FACING IN THIS LIFE?

We Will Trust Him Still

WEEK THREE · DAY FOUR

Psalm 44 is a prayer of praise and a prayer of honest petition. The nation of Israel was fighting battles, and they were not having victory. The psalm recounts God's covenant faithfulness to His people. They remember what had been taught to them by their fathers and how God had put them in the promised land. The word used in verse 2 is "planted." It brings us back to Psalm 1 where we learned that the blessed man was planted by God. The same word is used here of God's people. The people of God are not like wild trees that grow wherever the wind takes the seed. God's people are chosen and planted right where He wants them, and they are carefully cultivated by a loving Father. How often we wonder just like Israel did why bad things happen if we are right where He wants us! This heartfelt psalm is quoted by Paul in the book of Romans, and we are given insight into these words. God welcomed their questions. He always desires for us to be honest and vulnerable before Him. Tim Keller says that God wants us to come to Him with "uncensored hearts." But as we look at Romans 8:31-39, we are reminded that God is for us and that there is nothing that can separate us from His love.

In Christ, even what seems like a defeat is actually a victory. We may not understand what He is doing, but we can be assured that He is fighting for us. He has promised to work all for our good (Romans 8:28), and we can rest in confidence that His way is perfect (Psalm 18:30). There is nothing we can trust more than Him. As David said in Psalm 20:7, some trust in horses and some in chariots, but we are going to trust our God. We are going to trust that He knows what is best and that He can see what we cannot see. We will even say like Job, "Though he slay me, I will hope in him" (Job 13:15). We will remember the words of Jesus who told us that in this world we would face tribulation, but we can take heart because He has overcome the world (John 16:33). We don't follow God so that everything in life will be easy—we follow Him because we get God. He is enough no matter what happens. And even my trials are part of His faithful plan for me. May we have the faith to believe that He is working for us!

WHAT DOES IT MEAN THAT WE HAVE BEEN PLANTED AS GOD'S PEOPLE?
WE SEE THIS WORD REFERENCED IN VERSE 2 AND ALSO IN PSALM 1.

READ ROMANS 8:31-39. WHAT COMFORT DOES THIS GIVE TO BELIEVERS?

HOW CAN SOMETHING THAT SEEMS LIKE A DEFEAT ACTUALLY BE A VICTORY?

My Heart Overflows

WEEK THREE · DAY FIVE

The psalmist begins Psalm 45 with the declaration that his heart *overflows*. And isn't this the position of our hearts as well? We are overwhelmed by His goodness and overwhelmed by who our God is. This beautiful messianic psalm is first and foremost a song of praise about Jesus our Messiah, God, and King. Some believe that it speaks of Solomon as well, and though it may, it most definitely points to the One who is greater than Solomon (Matthew 12:42). Though Solomon was wise, Jesus is the source of all wisdom and knowledge (Colossians 2:3).

This psalm is a heavenly love song. It is a love song of the Messiah and His people, and it gives us a beautiful glimpse of the church. This psalm is quoted of Jesus in Hebrews 1:8-9, and it is a powerful record of the full humanity and complete deity of Jesus as seen in verses 2 and 6. *Jesus is fully God and fully man.* This psalm is prophecy of Jesus and points toward Him as the Messiah to come. It speaks of who Jesus is. Charles Spurgeon beautifully stated that, "Jesus reveals himself when we are pouring forth our affections towards him." When we come to Him, He will reveal Himself (Jeremiah 29:13-14). We see a picture of who Jesus is written with words so beautiful, and yet that still leaves us trying to describe the beauty of who He is. His words are full of grace. He is our Warrior who fights for us and defeats our enemies. He is majestic, true, meek, and righteous. Verse 6 tells us that His throne is forever and ever, and the words mimic those spoken to the young Mary as she learned that the child she was carrying would reign forever and ever (Luke 1:30-33). It also points us to the words of Revelation 11:15 as we await the day we will worship Him and declare that He will reign forever. He is beautiful for us to look on. Though on earth Jesus was just a humble man, He will be robed in majesty for all eternity. He is anointed with the oil of gladness reserved for distinguished guests of honor. And we will share in it with Him (Isaiah 61:3).

Though on earth His robes are stripped from Him (John 19:23-24), for eternity He will be clothed in glory. The fragrance of His garment reminds us of how His sacrifice is a fragrant offering (Ephesians 5:2), and in Him we become the fragrance of Jesus (2 Corinthians 2:15). The psalm continues with a beautiful picture of Jesus as the bridegroom and His people as the bride. It is a poetic picture of the descriptions of the church in Ephesians 5:25-32, Revelation 19, and Revelation 22:17. And for all of time we as His people will worship Him. We will remember His name which is who He is and every aspect of His character, and we will worship—what else can we do for all that He has done for us?

WHAT PARTS OF GOD'S CHARACTER OVERWHELM YOUR HEART TO PRAISE?

WHAT CAN WE LEARN ABOUT JESUS FROM THIS PSALM?

HOW CAN WE CAUSE GOD'S NAME TO BE
REMEMBERED BY THOSE AROUND US?

SEND YOUR LIGHT

AND YOUR TRUTH;

LET THEM LEAD ME.

LET THEM BRING ME TO

YOUR HOLY MOUNTAIN,

TO YOUR DWELLING PLACE.

Psalm 43:3

WEEK THREE

Weekly Reflection ——————————————————————

Read Psalm 41-45

HOW DOES THIS PASSAGE POINT TO THE GOSPEL?

HOW SHOULD YOU RESPOND TO THIS PASSAGE?
WHAT IS THE PERSONAL APPLICATION?

WHAT SPECIFIC ACTION STEPS CAN YOU TAKE
THIS WEEK TO APPLY THE PASSAGE?

Be Still and Know

WEEK FOUR · DAY ONE

God is our refuge and strength. The start of this beautiful psalm pulls us in with its first words. The psalm speaks of the absolute confidence we can have in our God. The psalm was possibly written by Hezekiah about God's deliverance of His people from Assyria. The psalm states a powerful truth in verse 1, that God is our refuge or shelter, and He is our strength. He is close to us in times of trouble. Because of this truth, we have nothing to fear. No matter what comes, we can trust the Lord. The examples are extreme—the end of the earth, the greatest mountains being thrown into the sea, roaring waters, and trembling mountains. Yet God's people have no reason to fear. His steadfast love remains through it all (Isaiah 54:10). We can trust Him even if the worst possible thing we could imagine happened.

In ancient times, one of the greatest fears was that the water supply would be compromised. But God promises a river to His people. *He* is the river. The river of His grace refreshes and sustains us. He is the water of life for the thirsty (Psalm 36:8, 65:9, 87:7, John 4:13-14, John 7:37-39, Revelation 22:17). God dwells with His people (John 1:14). He is in their midst. Nothing can move us, shake us, or separate us from our God (Romans 8:37-39). All He has to do is say the word and the world obeys. He is with us. He is our Immanuel.

In verse 1, the word for refuge means "shelter," and in verse 7 the word means "high tower." He is both for us. Our shelter right in the midst of trouble, and He is our high tower that lifts us high above the cares of the world. We are called to come and behold what He has done. He will never let us down. In verse 10, we are given a call to be still. We are being commanded to stop trying to do it in our own strength and abide in Him (John 15). The Hebrew here literally means that we need to let go, relax, and let the cares of this life fall from our grasp. This is rich truth for us. Being still isn't about a relaxing morning, it is about relaxing and resting our anxious hearts. It is about taking our hands off of our situation and placing it in His hands. It is about holding our life with open hands instead of a white-knuckled grip. It is about trusting Him. We are still before Him, by knowing who He is. This knowledge is not just intellectual. This is knowledge by experience. Knowing who He is enables us to surrender to Him. We can surrender to Him because we know His character and faithfulness. What a reminder for us to open His Word and learn who He is so our hearts can be stilled before Him.

HOW DOES THE TRUTH OF GOD'S WORD DRIVE
AWAY FEAR FROM OUR HEARTS?

WHY CAN WE TRUST HIM EVEN IF THE WORST POSSIBLE THING HAPPENED?

WHAT DOES IT MEAN TO BE STILL?

Sing Praises to Our God

WEEK FOUR · DAY TWO

This messianic psalm teaches us how and why we should praise the Lord. The stillness before the Lord in Psalm 46:10 gives way to joyful praise for who He is. God's people should be characterized and known for our joy. With all that God has done for us, how could we be miserable people? This response of worship comes from all peoples and is a poignant reminder of how God is calling His children from every tribe, tongue, and nation. It was to Abraham that God promised that through his seed all nations of the earth would be blessed (Genesis 12:1-3). Jesus is the fulfillment of that prophecy. He is the Messiah who would open wide the arms of salvation to all. The psalmist would look forward to His coming, but he speaks as if it is already done. God's promises are sure, and if God has promised it, it is as good as done.

He is the great king in battles, and He is our mighty warrior. The problems and situations that we face are not too difficult for Him to handle. Verse 4 tells us that He chose our heritage, or inheritance, for us. Just as He did for the tribes of Israel, He has chosen our inheritance as well. For all of God's people, He Himself is our inheritance, and we are His chosen people. But He also chooses our circumstances, and though we don't always understand His plan, we can trust Him. There is no need for us to be discontent or to look at what He has given to someone else. We can be assured that He has given us what is best for us. We can surrender fully to Him because we are assured of His love for us. He loves us because of His grace, not because of anything that we have done (Ephesians 2:8-9). We see the words "sing praises" repeated five times, and the repetition shows us how important these words are. In Hebrew this is one word. It reflects both the action and the heart behind the action. When we realize that this is one word repeated over and over, it shows us just how important it is for us to pour out our hearts to our God. We praise the one who sits in authority on the throne. We worship the God who has people from every nation bowing before Him. We worship the One who even nature itself points to, the one God revealed to us in three persons in the Father, Son, and Holy Spirit. He is the Lord of the whole earth, and the Lord of our hearts. We bow our hearts before Him.

HOW IS JESUS A FULFILLMENT OF THIS MESSIANIC PSALM,
AS WELL AS GENESIS 12:1-3?

HOW CAN WE REST IN THE TRUTH THAT HE HAS
CHOSEN OUR CIRCUMSTANCES?

READ PSALM 16 AS A REMINDER OF HOW HIS CHOICE FOR US IS GOOD.
WHY DOES BEING ASSURED OF HIS LOVE ALLOW US TO SURRENDER?
WHAT DO YOU NEED TO SURRENDER TODAY?

Think About His Love

WEEK FOUR · DAY THREE

We serve a great and holy God, and it is in looking at Him that we gain confidence to face this life. Charles Spurgeon said, "Where God is most seen, He is best loved." Our study of Scripture should always be to help us see Him and love Him more. This psalm begins with a reminder of His greatness. We see a picture of Zion, or Jerusalem. We are pointed forward to think on the new Zion, but we also remember as we study this beautiful psalm that God dwells with us and in us now. We are the city and dwelling place of God. Jerusalem is spoken of as the beautiful city on a hill, and Jesus tells those who believe that we are to shine His light as a city set on a hill (Matthew 5:14-16). Jerusalem will always be the joy of the whole earth because it was there that our Savior died, making payment for our sin, and it was there that He rose again, bringing hope for all the world.

This same God dwells in His people and is with His church. He is fighting for His people and making Himself known. In verse 8, we see words that remind us that He has been faithful. He has done what He has promised. And this city will be established forever. God's chosen people show a picture of that, and the new Jerusalem will be established forever with full restoration as a place where there is no more crying, tears, sorrow, or death (Revelation 21).

So, as verse 9 states, we will think on His love. We will dwell on that steadfast, hesed love. Matthew Henry said, " All the streams of God's mercy that flow down to us must be traced up to the foundation of God's lovingkindness." Our God loves us, and His love has changed the course of our life. He loved us while we were still sinners (Romans 5:8), and He has shown us His steadfast love and grace. God is our refuge. He is our strong tower. This is who He is. He is holy, just, merciful, loving, faithful, gracious, and so much more. Yet He calls us by name. He is not just God—He is *our* God. Let those words settle into your heart. He will lead us and guide us forever. Some versions end with, "even unto death." He will be with us every step of the way. We have nothing to fear because of who He is.

WHY SHOULD WE STUDY SCRIPTURE TO KNOW MORE OF WHO GOD IS?

HOW DOES WHO GOD IS IMPACT OUR DAILY LIVES?
HOW DOES THINKING ON HIS LOVE CHANGE OUR PERSPECTIVE?

SPEND A FEW MOMENTS MEDITATING ON WHO GOD IS.
WRITE SOME OF THEM DOWN BELOW.

What Will I Trust In?

WEEK FOUR · DAY TWO

We are all trusting in something. We can trust in the Lord, or we can trust in ourselves. This proverbial or didactic psalm is meant to teach us about what matters most. The psalm begins with a call to all people to listen to these words. Leaders and peasants. Rich and poor. Men or women. This is for the nobodies and the somebodies. It is for everyone. Money is a necessary part of life. It is something that we all think about to some degree. Some are wealthy and think about how to get more; others have very little and also focus on the desire for more. We view money as a kind of security net, but the security of money is not true security. Money is not bad, but when we begin to depend on money instead of on the Lord, we have a problem. There is nothing wrong with having money, and there is not even anything sinful about having a lot of money, but when our focus is on money, we need to refocus our hearts on the Lord. An obsession with money can happen to both those that have a lot and to those that have a little. Over and over throughout the psalm, we are reminded of the foolishness (or folly as Proverbs would call it) of trusting in money and of the wisdom of trusting the Lord. We must set our hearts on the things that are above (Colossians 3:2).

We serve a God with an upside-down kingdom where the last are first and the first are last. And just like the story of the rich young ruler (Matthew 19:16-30), God wants us to place our trust in Him and not our money. We don't need to keep up with the Joneses, but instead, follow Jesus. For those that do not follow God, they are led by their money, and their shepherd is death. But for the believer, we are led by God, and the Lord Himself is our Shepherd (Psalm 23). This is a comfort for God's people. Though there is judgment for sin and those that choose to follow money and self, God will ransom His people. Whether we have much or little on this earth, we can lay up treasures in heaven (Matthew 6:19-21). We can invest in His unshakable kingdom.

WHAT THINGS DO YOU OFTEN TRUST IN?

WHY DOES MONEY SO OFTEN DISTRACT US FROM THE LORD?

WHY ARE THE THINGS YOU OFTEN TRUST IN INFERIOR
TO TRUSTING IN THE LORD?

Heart of Worship

WEEK FOUR · DAY FIVE

What does the Lord desire from His people? In this psalm, we hear from God what He desires. The psalm opens with three names of God from the start. We see El, Elohim, and Yahweh. We are seeing that God is both the almighty and powerful God as well as the personal and covenant God of His people. We see His majestic description of His glory, and we also see the truth that He cares for us. Our God is both transcendent above us and Immanuel, God with us. We view both the shining of His glory and the consuming fire of His holiness. Both were seen at the giving of the law and here again (Exodus 24:17, Deuteronomy 33:2).

Beginning in verse 7, God speaks to His people. He is pleading with His own and reminding them that He is their God. Again, this is something that was done at the giving of the law as God said that He was the Lord who brought them out of Egypt (Exodus 20:2). God reminds them of who He is but also of who they are as His covenant people. His message to His people is the heart of this psalm. God did not just want sacrifice without a heart of worship. God wants transformed hearts, not simply outward conformity. The gospel is not one of moralism. The gospel overwhelms us in grace and transforms from the inside out. *God wants us.* This is the message to the people of God. He wants our hearts more than our outward service and sacrifice. This truth is all throughout Scripture (Hosea 6:6, 1 Samuel 15:22, Amos 5:21-24, Micah 6:6-8, Mark 12:28-34). God desires love and obedience from hearts overflowing with gratitude instead of people doing what they are supposed to out of obligation. God reminds them that He already owns it all, even the sacrificial animals. He doesn't need our sacrifice, but He desires our surrender. Verse 14 tells us what God wants from His people. He desires thankfulness, obedience, and prayer. Only God can enable us to live this way. It is not our own strength but Him working in our hearts and us yielding to Him in faith. How interesting that God says that what He wants more than sacrifice is us *asking* in prayer. He would rather us ask than give because He wants us to recognize that we need Him. Even our prayer becomes an offering of worship when it comes from a surrendered heart. God speaks to those who practice wickedness and urges them to turn to Him. He reminds them that there is truly none like Him. The psalm ends with one more reminder of what He desires from the people that He loves. He desires everything that we do to overflow from a heart of love and gratitude. *He wants our hearts.* He wants our surrender. He wants us to recognize our need so that He can satisfy us with Himself.

SOMETIMES WE ARE TEMPTED TO JUST CONFORM OUR OUTWARD APPEARANCE AND ACTIONS. WHY DOES GOD DESIRE SOMETHING MORE FROM US?

WHAT DO YOU NEED TO SURRENDER?

HOW DOES RECOGNIZING OUR NEED LEAD TO GREATER SATISFACTION?

GOD IS OUR REFUGE
AND STRENGTH,
A HELPER WHO IS
ALWAYS FOUND
IN TIMES OF TROUBLE.

Psalm 46:1

WEEK FOUR

Weekly Reflection —————————

Read Psalm 46-50

PARAPHRASE THE PASSAGE FROM THIS WEEK.

WHAT DID YOU OBSERVE FROM THIS WEEK'S TEXT
ABOUT GOD AND HIS CHARACTER?

WHAT DOES THE PASSAGE TEACH ABOUT THE CONDITION OF MANKIND
AND ABOUT YOURSELF?

HOW DOES THIS PASSAGE POINT TO THE GOSPEL?

HOW SHOULD YOU RESPOND TO THIS PASSAGE?
WHAT IS THE PERSONAL APPLICATION?

WHAT SPECIFIC ACTION STEPS CAN YOU TAKE
THIS WEEK TO APPLY THE PASSAGE?

Create in Me
a Clean Heart

WEEK FIVE • DAY ONE

David was a man after God's own heart, and yet he was not immune to sin. This psalm is a prayer of David after he was confronted by Nathan the prophet for his sin. He had not only committed adultery with Bathsheba, but he had her husband, Uriah, murdered as well by commanding him to the front line of the battle. 2 Samuel 11-12 gives the full context of this psalm.

As David sees his sin, he cries out to the Lord for mercy. David had let his sin go on for too long, and now he prays and pleads God's character. He prays for God to be who He is and asks Him to demonstrate His mercy and steadfast love. He wants God to cleanse him and blot out his transgressions (Colossians 2:14). He wanted every single part of himself to be cleansed. Every thought, every action, every motive. He wasn't going to hold anything back. Spurgeon said, "When we deal generously with our sin, God will deal gently with us." We must see the weight of our sin and take it to the Lord. David said his sin was ever before him. He felt the weight of conviction. Conviction is a gift. It is a gift because the Spirit gently reveals our need and also points us to our Savior. David recognized who he was and what he had done. He recognized that all sin is against the Lord. He also recognized that he was both a sinner by nature and by choice. He wept over his fallen condition. These verses remind us of Matthew 5:4, "Blessed are those who mourn, for they shall be comforted." God's comfort can only come to those who have mourned their need.

God didn't just want outward conformity but transformed hearts. David prayed for cleansing. We find a mention here of hyssop which was a bush used to sprinkle blood and water for ceremonial cleansing. It is also what was used to apply the blood to the doorposts during the Passover (Exodus 12:22). We are cleansed from our sin by the blood of Jesus (1 John 1:9, Hebrews 10:22), and we are made whiter than snow (Isaiah 1:18). David prayed for God to create a new heart in him. We have no power to make our hearts clean—it must be God in us. David prayed for a new heart to be created in him (Ezekiel 11:19-20, 36:26-28). We become a new creation at salvation, but our sanctification is a process of asking Him to recreate and restore us. We ask Him to make us like Him.

There is a shift at the end of the psalm as David asks to be made new so that he can point others to the Lord. Our heart's desire should be to use every part of our story, even our mistakes, to point others to the Lord. God desires changed hearts and not just sacrifices (Psalm 50), and as we come to Him, we can ask Him to make us clean. We don't have to be good enough to earn His favor. The beauty of the gospel is that we come to Him weak and He transforms us with His strength.

GOD WANTS TRANSFORMED HEARTS AND NOT JUST OUTWARD CONFORMITY. HOW ARE WE SOMETIMES TEMPTED TO JUST CONFORM OUR ACTIONS AND NOT OUR HEARTS?

WHY IS IT A COMFORTING TRUTH THAT WE DON'T HAVE THE POWER TO TRANSFORM OURSELVES?

HOW DOES 2 CORINTHIANS 12:9-10 REINFORCE THE TRUTH THAT GOD CAN USE EVEN OUR WEAKNESS TO POINT TO HIS STRENGTH?

Flourish

WEEK FIVE · DAY TWO

Psalm 52 is a psalm of David, and we are told that it was written when Doeg betrayed David and told Saul where he was. You can read the full story in 1 Samuel 21:1-9, 22:6-23. David was with the priest Ahimelech when Doeg sees him, and Doeg reports back to Saul. Saul not only stays on the hunt for David, but kills Ahimelech the priest and the other priests that day. This account and this psalm remind us that sin and pride always take you farther than you plan to go. Saul had once been anointed by God and crowned king, and yet now he was not only searching for David, but he also killed 85 priests. Both Saul and Doeg were men who trusted in their own strength, power, and wealth.

We can find so much comfort in the second line of this psalm. God's steadfast love endures all the day—even when things seem really bad. This is hope for the one that follows the Lord, and it is hope for the sinner. *His mercy has not run out.* He is the One we can turn to. We can come to Him and lay down our sin and pride. We can find rest in Him. We see a further description of the wicked as one who plots and speaks evil. How often we also speak words that we know will hurt. Sometimes hurtful words are careless words, but other times, we know exactly what we are doing when we use our speech to put others down and build ourselves up. We must examine our own hearts. In this examining, we must look at the things that occupy our minds and fills our thoughts. And as we examine our hearts, we must fall on His grace. God will judge in righteousness. He will not ignore evil. So we must make Him alone our refuge and trust in Him and not ourselves (Psalm 46:1-3).

Verse 8 begins the contrast of the righteous who is not uprooted by the wicked (v5), but who is like a flourishing olive tree. The olive tree produced abundant fruit. It flourished. David's throne would be established forever because of Jesus. And David would praise as if it was already done (v.9) because that is just how faithful God is. He would do what He had promised to do. We can come to Him with confidence no matter what we may face in our day or in our life. We know that He will be faithful. We know that He will do what He has promised. We can wait for Him with expectation because He is the faithful God.

WHY DO WE FIND COMFORT IN THE TRUTH THAT GOD IS IN CONTROL EVEN WHEN THINGS DON'T MAKE SENSE TO US?

HOW DO WE USE OUR WORDS TO HURT OTHER PEOPLE?

GOD'S PROMISES ARE AS GOOD AS DONE — HE WILL BE FAITHFUL. HOW DOES THIS CHANGE YOUR PERSPECTIVE ON YOUR LIFE?

Grace Abounds

WEEK FIVE · DAY THREE

Psalm 53 is very closely related to Psalm 14, and the fact that these words are repeated reminds us of how important they are. We must be aware of our deep need before we can see the glory of salvation. We need the reminder that it was while we were yet sinners and enemies of God that Jesus died for us (Romans 5:6-8). It was not because of any good that we had done, but only by His grace. The fool says in his heart that there is no God, and this is the state of every unbeliever. We must also take a long hard look at our own sin as well because this not only speaks to intellectual atheism, but to practical atheism. The Hebrew here is "no god." For the unbeliever, this may come across as, "God is not for me," or "I am not into religion." But for the believer, it can come across as us thinking that our way, plan, or timing is better than God's. It manifests itself in us trying to live in our own strength when the truth of the matter is that we cannot take even a breath without Him. May we never live in a state of practical atheism where we live as if there is no God. And when we catch ourselves trying to do things on our own, may we return to Him quickly.

Much of what is seen here regarding the state of man is quoted in Romans 3. And we are reminded that though we do not seek Him or have any righteousness of our own, He sought us. We are utterly hopeless without Him. But this is the beauty of the gospel—that He sought us. We cannot see the beauty of the gospel if we never see the weight of our sin or the depth of our depravity. But for those of us who have placed our faith in His grace, we have nothing to fear. God will defeat our enemies. He will come through for us.

David prayed verse 6 as he looked ahead to the first advent and the coming of Jesus who would bring salvation out of Zion as He was sacrificed at the cross for us. He also looked forward to the second advent that we await now. We wait for the coming restoration when all will be made right (Revelation 21). How we praise Him for salvation and the truth that where sin abounded, grace abounded all the more (Romans 5:20). His grace is full and free, and it is more than enough.

HOW DO PEOPLE LIVE AS IF THERE IS NO GOD?

HOW CAN WE LIVE DIFFERENTLY?

READ ROMANS 3:10-20 AND FEEL THE WEIGHT OF OUR CONDITION WITHOUT CHRIST. NOW CONTINUE READING ROMANS 3:21-26 AND SEE THE REDEMPTION FOUND IN JESUS ALONE. SUMMARIZE THE MESSAGE OF ROMANS 3:10-26. HOW IS VERSE 6 FULFILLED AT THE CROSS? HOW WILL IT ULTIMATELY BE FULFILLED WHEN JESUS COMES AGAIN?

He Has Done it

WEEK FIVE · DAY FOUR

In this psalm, we again find David under attack. He has been betrayed by the Ziphites who revealed his location to Saul. David does the only thing he can do, and it is a reminder to ask what we must do when trouble comes to us as well. The first line sets before us the plea of David as he runs to God alone who is his salvation. There is nowhere we can turn but to our God. He alone can rescue us. David's prayer is that God will be who He is. David pleads on behalf of God's name. This is the sum total of His character. David is saying, "you are faithful—be faithful to me. You are just—be just to me." His prayer is that God will hear and that God will act.

He does hear, and He will answer. He hears every prayer uttered from our lips, and He hears every groaning of our hearts. It didn't matter how many people came against David; God was with him and would not forsake him. First glance showed enemies all around, but a closer look through the eyes of faith showed that God was very present in the situation that may have felt hopeless. So often our circumstances can keep us from seeing God who is right there with us. Our sorrow can blind us to his presence, but He has not gone anywhere.

When it seems impossible, look again. When it seems evil will win, look again. When it feels like you are all alone, look again.
He has not left your side. He will bring justice, and we do not have to try to bring justice on our own. He will be faithful. He will keep His promises.

The psalm closes with a freewill offering. This is spontaneous, voluntary praise. This is worship, not because it is what is expected or required, but because our hearts are utterly overflowing with who he is. He is *good*. The psalm ends with a declaration that David has been delivered from every trouble. In his life, David would still base trouble and hardship on his knowledge that God was with him. With our God, His promises are as good as done. David could praise God in confidence, and with expectant hope. We can do the same. We can be assured that He will do what He has promised. He has already done it. It is as good as done.

WHAT IS OUR FIRST REACTION WHEN TROUBLES COME?

WHAT SHOULD OUR REACTION TO TROUBLES BE?

WRITE DOWN SOME VERSES THAT YOU CAN LOOK AT WHEN YOU ARE GOING THROUGH A DIFFICULT TIME. HERE ARE A FEW REFERENCES TO GET YOU STARTED: PSALM 34:18, PSALM 73:26, PSALM 62:8, 2 CORINTHIANS 12:9, ROMANS 8:28, PROVERBS 3:5-6, I PETER 5:7. TAKE NOTE OF HOW VERSE 7 STATES THAT GOD HAS DELIVERED DAVID. IN THE CONTEXT OF THIS PSALM, DAVID WOULD STILL FACE MUCH HARDSHIP AFTER WRITING THIS, BUT HE KNEW THAT GOD WOULD DO WHAT HE HAS PROMISED. WHAT PROMISE FROM SCRIPTURE DO YOU NEED TO CLAIM TODAY?

He Will Sustain You

WEEK FIVE · DAY FIVE

This psalm of David is one that shows great suffering and the even greater sustaining hand of God. It is thought by many to be a messianic psalm that reminds us of the sufferings of Jesus. In this psalm, David is at a low place. He has been betrayed by those closest to him. All he can do is cry out to the Lord. The psalm begins with David pleading for God to listen, to be present, to come near, and to answer. David pours out his situation before the Lord and comes to God with raw vulnerability. We can come to God in this same way, pouring our heart out before Him. So often as David did, we want to run from our problems. We search everywhere else for shelter, but shelter is found only in the Lord.

David pleads for God's justice to reign. He comes to the Lord and pours out his heart with confidence that God will hear him. How differently we would view our problems if we only remembered that God is near!

He can redeem anything. *Anything.* He can bring abundant life from our deepest sorrow. Suffering pushes us to the Lord. It reminds us of our need. It reminds us of the truth of the gospel that we can't do it on our own. Matt Chandler said, "The message of Scripture and the gospel of Jesus Christ is not that in following him everything goes right, but that he is enough no matter what happens." *Jesus is enough.* No matter what. Jesus is enough. Other people may fail us and betray us, but He never will. Others may violate their covenants, but He is our covenant-keeping God. We can cast our burdens and anxieties on Him alone (1 Peter 5:7). We can be confident that He will never allow us to be shaken or moved. We are secure in Him alone, and we can trust Him. No matter what we are facing, we must run to Him. When our situation feels hopeless, we will hope in Him. When our burdens are too heavy for us, we will give them to Him. We will trust that He will redeem even this. Because when nothing else makes sense, He does.

WHAT ARE SOME THINGS IN YOUR LIFE THAT IT FEELS HARD TO IMAGINE
GOD COULD REDEEM? CAN YOU TRUST HIM TO REDEEM EVERYTHING,
 EVEN THESE THINGS?

WHAT THREE WORDS WOULD YOU USE TO DESCRIBE THIS PSALM?

HOW CAN YOU TRUST HIM THIS WEEK? WRITE OUT A PRAYER
OF CONFIDENCE IN GOD NO MATTER WHAT.

GOD, CREATE A
CLEAN HEART FOR ME
AND RENEW A STEADFAST
SPIRIT WITHIN ME.

Psalm 51:10

WEEK FIVE

Weekly Reflection —————————————————————————

Read Psalm 51-55

PARAPHRASE THE PASSAGE FROM THIS WEEK.

WHAT DID YOU OBSERVE FROM THIS WEEK'S TEXT ABOUT GOD AND HIS CHARACTER?

WHAT DOES THE PASSAGE TEACH ABOUT THE CONDITION OF MANKIND AND ABOUT YOURSELF?

HOW DOES THIS PASSAGE POINT TO THE GOSPEL?

HOW SHOULD YOU RESPOND TO THIS PASSAGE?
WHAT IS THE PERSONAL APPLICATION?

WHAT SPECIFIC ACTION STEPS CAN YOU TAKE
THIS WEEK TO APPLY THE PASSAGE?

Fear and Faith

WEEK SIX · DAY ONE

In this psalm, which was written around the same time as Psalm 34 and when David had fled to Gath (1 Samuel 21), we see David wrestle with fear and faith. There is a tension of fear and faith in the life of the believer. We must remember like David that though our enemies are strong, our God is stronger. David comes to the Lord in need. He is coming to God for help. He comes honestly before the Lord and recognizes his own fear and weakness. He does not pretend to have it all together, and yet he asks God to be with him. It is reminiscent of the man in Mark who said, "I believe, help my unbelief" (Mark 9:24).

There will be times of fear, and waiting, and uncertainty, and it is then that we must run to the Lord. The life of faith is one of trusting even when the situation seems impossible. Warren Wiersbe said, "Faith is living without scheming." How quick we are to scheme and to try to do things on our own, and yet our God calls us to be still and trust him. Even when things seem impossible, we can be confident that there is nothing that can separate us from the love of God (Romans 8:31-39). If God is for us, who can be against us? There is no one and nothing that can stand against. We are secure in Him.

Verse 8 reminds us that our God knows every ache of our heart and sees every tear that we shed. He sees every step we take, and He is with us through it all. He weeps with us and comforts us in our sufferings. What a comfort that He has forgotten our sins but remembered our tears. He is the faithful one who will not abandon us. Verse 9 reminds us that God is for us. *He is for me. He is on my side. He is fighting my battles.* Our faith is strengthened by the battle. We grow as we learn to run to Him. We learned that faith is stronger than fear because our faith is in the One who is stronger than anything.

READ I SAMUEL 21:10-15. SOMETIMES WE FORGET THAT THE BIBLE CHARACTERS WERE REAL PEOPLE WITH REAL STRUGGLES AND EMOTIONS. THIS PSALM WAS WRITTEN AT A VERY LOW POINT IN DAVID'S LIFE. HE IS WRESTLING WITH FEAR AND FAITH. HOW CAN THESE WORDS COMFORT YOU WHEN YOU FACE A DIFFICULT SEASON?

SOMETIMES IN THE FACE OF VERY STRONG ENEMIES, WE FORGET THAT OUR GOD IS SO MUCH STRONGER. WHAT ARE SOME THINGS THAT YOU CAN DO TO REMIND YOURSELF OF WHO GOD IS IN YOUR DAILY LIFE? LIST OUT SOME OF THE ASPECTS OF GOD'S CHARACTER BELOW THAT REMIND YOU THAT GOD IS STRONGER THAN YOUR ENEMY.

IN WHAT WAYS ARE YOU TEMPTED TO "SCHEME," OR TRY TO CONTROL YOUR OWN LIFE INSTEAD OF TRUSTING THE LORD? LIST OUT SOME AREAS THAT YOU NEED TO TRUST HIM IN THIS WEEK.

Let Your Glory Cover The Earth

WEEK SIX · DAY TWO

This psalm was written as David fled from Saul and hid in a cave. It was an unlikely place for the man anointed to be king, and yet even there, David clung to the Lord. The psalm begins with a prayer for mercy as David pours out his heart and his situation to the Lord. God already knows every thought of our hearts and everything that we face, and yet He delights in us coming to Him. David recognizes that his only refuge was in God. He finds refuge under the wings of God, which is a reference to the wings of the cherubim and over the holy of holies. It illustrates definitely for us that our places of suffering can be transformed to places of worship in the presence of God. His presence transforms. David could rest even in the midst of the storm because he knew the Master of the storm. David knew that God would faithfully fulfill His purpose, and we can have the same assurance. Our God works His plans for us even through suffering. Like David, we can boldly declare in faith that we will trust our God. When the situation looks bleak, we can place our hope in the One who is working all things for the good of His people (Romans 8:28). The repetition in verse 3 reminds us that He will—He will do it. Our God will be faithful to us. And even when the situation looks hopeless, we can hope in Him. Verse 5 brings out what is the chorus of the song. It is also repeated in verse 11. It is a call for God's exultation and God's glory to be over all the earth. We often speak of Gods glory, but what is it? God's glory is who He is. It is the sum of His character put on display. So we pray for His glory to be revealed. Even in trials, David could pray in confidence with a steadfastly fixed heart that said, no matter what, *I will love God. I will serve God. I will trust God. I will worship God.* When we get just a glimpse of God's glory, we will have the same confident trust.

In verse 8 we see a prayer for awakening. David prays for his own glory to awake. He is saying that he wants to worship with every part of who he is. Because no matter how bad things may appear, we can be utterly convinced of who God is. The song ends with the repeat of the chorus and the cry of God's people for the glory of God to be revealed. How similar to the Lord's prayer and pleading for "Your kingdom come, Your will be done. On earth as it is in heaven" (Matthew 6:10). Let your glory cover the earth, Lord!

THE WORD "WILL" IS REPEATED SEVERAL TIMES IN THIS PSALM. SOMETIMES WE SEE WHAT GOD WILL DO, AND OTHER TIMES WE SEE WHAT DAVID (AND WE) WILL OR SHOULD DO. READ THE PSALM AGAIN AND LOOK FOR THOSE REPEATED WORDS. WHAT DO THOSE STATEMENTS TELL YOU ABOUT WHO GOD IS AND HOW WE SHOULD RESPOND TO HIM?

READ THE LORD'S PRAYER IN MATTHEW 6:9-13. WHAT SIMILARITIES DO YOU SEE BETWEEN THIS PSALM AND THE PRAYER?

HOW SHOULD THESE THINGS CHANGE THE WAY THAT WE PRAY?

There is None Like Him

WEEK SIX · DAY THREE

In this psalm of David, David laments the unjust leaders of the world. This psalm is heavy for us to read, but it is not about revenge. It is about a desire for justice and the desire for good to conquer evil. This isn't about getting our way, but about giving God glory. This psalm is a reminder that there is none like Him (Jeremiah 10:6, Psalm 86:8). Only He is righteous. Only He is just. Only He is holy. Only He is merciful. Only He is gracious. Only He is God. This psalm looks at the condition of mankind without God, and then it pushes us to look to God. Look at this world, and then look to the One who is so much greater than this world.

These words are reminders for us to not get comfortable with sin or get used to evil. We should be saddened by the results of the fall. This should push us to gratitude for what God has done for us and give us a fervency in sharing the gospel. David prayed for God to bring justice, and he did not take things into his own hands. God is the one that judges—not us. We must remember this truth. God's way, not our way. God's timing, not our timing. Though man's life is like a vapor, our God is everlasting. We can trust Him to do what is right at the perfect time.

These words are hard for us to read. Ask God to show Himself. As we see His glory and His holiness, we will see the weight and the seriousness of our sin. We are not likely to put these words on a coffee mug, but they are God's words so we must ask God to help our hearts understand them. He is just and righteous. He extends mercy and grace and pleads with us to take this gift of His mercy. For now, we live in His grace, and we share it with all that we meet. We await the day when evil will be defeated, and we will see our Savior face-to-face. Judgment for sin is hard to read. But our hearts wait in anticipation for the day when evil will be defeated, when sin and death will be no more, and when Jesus will wipe away every tear. We can trust our God to do what is right.

READ JEREMIAH 10:6 AND PSALM 86:8. WRITE DOWN SOME WAYS THAT THERE IS NONE LIKE GOD. HOW IS GOD DIFFERENT THAN US?

GOD IS HOLY AND RIGHTEOUS AND MUST BRING JUSTICE FOR EVIL. ROMANS 3:10-18 REMINDS US OF OUR FALLEN AND SINFUL CONDITION. HOW DOES THIS MAKE US STAND IN AWE OF THE GRACE THAT HAS BEEN EXTENDED TO US IN SALVATION? READ EPHESIANS 2:1-10 TO BE REMINDED OF WHAT GOD HAS DONE FOR THOSE THAT HAVE PLACED THEIR FAITH IN JESUS FOR SALVATION.

AT THE END OF A PSALM THAT IS DIFFICULT TO READ BECAUSE OF ITS HEAVINESS COMES A PROMISE THAT GOD WILL REWARD THE RIGHTEOUS. WHAT DOES THIS PSALM TELL US ABOUT WHO GOD IS?

I Will Watch Over You

WEEK SIX • DAY FOUR

This psalm of lament was written while David was running for his life from Saul's men who were trying to kill him (1 Samuel 19:11-12). David was facing some very real enemies. He cried out to God for deliverance. He calls God, "my God," and it is a reminder of how personal and very powerful God is. Charles Spurgeon said, "God is our God, and therefore deliverance and defense are ours." We have a strong enemy, but we have a God who is stronger. What a privilege to be able to call to the Lord in prayer and know that He will hear and He will answer.

Verse 8 is a reminder that God is not afraid of His enemies. They do not scare or intimidate Him. What a great assurance that we put our trust in the One who is more powerful than any enemy that may stand against us. While his enemies were looking for ways to attack, David was looking for God to work. Verse 9 shows us that David was watching and waiting for God. David's enemies were waiting for David's downfall, but David was waiting for God. He said with confidence that God in His steadfast *hesed* love would meet him and would bring victory. When our enemy is attacking, or when life circumstances are bad, we can have that same confidence as we watch and wait for the Lord. We can pray, "Lord, I don't know what You are doing, but I am watching for you." We can have confidence that He is working even when we cannot see.

The end of the psalm is a declaration of faith. David chooses to praise God even when nothing around him made sense. Just as each morning is a reminder of fresh mercies (Lamentations 3:22-23), David poured out fresh praise to God. He adores God for who He is and what He has done. God is our strength, and our refuge, and our fortress. We will cling to His strength and not our own. When our enemies are all around, we will praise Him. We will see His steadfast love no matter what our situation, and we get to watch for His working.

THERE IS VICTORY TO BE FOUND IN OUR GOD. READ IN DEUTERONOMY 20:4 ABOUT HOW OUR GOD FIGHTS FOR US. THEN READ HOW JESUS HAS OVERCOME THE WORLD IN JOHN 16:33. HOW DO THESE VERSES ENCOURAGE YOU ABOUT WHATEVER YOU ARE FACING IN YOUR LIFE?

LOOK UP THE WORD "WATCH." WRITE OUT THE DEFINITION HERE AND EXPLAIN WHAT IT MEANS TO WATCH FOR THE LORD.

WE OFTEN DO NOT LIKE TO WAIT. BUT WAITING ISN'T SITTING AROUND DOING NOTHING; WAITING IN SCRIPTURE IS ACTIVE. IT IS TRUSTING GOD, EVEN WHEN THINGS DON'T HAPPEN IN OUR TIMING. IN THIS PSALM, WE SEE DAVID PRAISING GOD IN HIS SEASON OF WAITING. WHAT CAN YOU PRAISE GOD FOR TODAY?

Restore Us

In this psalm of lament, we are pointed again to our faithful God. So many times the people of Israel had wandered far from the Lord, and here in this psalm of David, we see God's people crying out to Him for restoration. Here we find the Hebrew word *Shuwb* that we have seen before. We see the same Hebrew word in Psalm 19:7 of God's Word, and of our own Good Shepherd in Psalm 23:3. God's people had faced hard things, but through it all, they had a place to turn. They had come to God in their weakness, longing for the strength that only He could give. In verse 4, we see the truth that God has given them a banner and a place to run to. Other parts of Scripture will show us that our God is this banner (Exodus 17:15), and the book of Hebrews will tell us that Jesus is the one to whom we flee for refuge (Hebrews 6:18-19).

In many ways, the gospel itself and the message of who our God is serves as the banner that we wave in every battle. David speaks of God's people as His beloved ones. What a comfort for us to know that our God who loves us with a covenant-keeping love calls us His beloved ones. So we come to Him and pray for Him to keep His promises. We find our hope in Him alone. We can see so clearly how God declares that all is His—all people and every nation. Yet He also pronounces judgment on those like Moab that have rejected His righteous rule. Israel was fighting physical battles, but we fight spiritual battles. Israel had material armor, and we have the armor of God to wage war against our enemy (Ephesians 6:10-20). The end of the psalm is a reminder of the victorious character of our God. He will do it. He will be victorious in righteousness. He is the victorious Lord. Our mission is not to go forward with the power of an army, but with the power of the gospel. We go to this world with His authority preaching the message of His kingdom (Matthew 28:18-20). And no matter what opposition may come, we know that victory is sure with the Victorious One on our side.

PART OF THE PRAYER OF THIS PSALM IS FOR GOD TO RESTORE US. THIS SAME HEBREW WORD IS USED IN PSALM 19:7 AS "REVIVE," AND PSALM 23:3. LOOK UP THIS WORD IN EITHER A HEBREW LEXICON, OR CONCORDANCE, OR IN AN ENGLISH DICTIONARY. WHAT DO YOU THINK IT MEANS FOR GOD TO RESTORE US, AND HOW DOES HE DO IT?

IN THIS PSALM, WE SEE THAT GOD IS GOD OVER EVERY NATION AND EVERY PERSON. HOW DOES THIS COMFORT US AS WE FACE THE CIRCUMSTANCES OF OUR OWN LIVES?

AS YOU THINK THROUGH THE PSALMS WE HAVE STUDIED, WHAT STANDS OUT TO YOU THE MOST? HOW CAN YOU TRUST GOD EVEN IN SEASONS OF WAITING? WHAT CHARACTER TRAITS OF GOD HAVE YOU SEEN AS YOU HAVE STUDIED THESE?

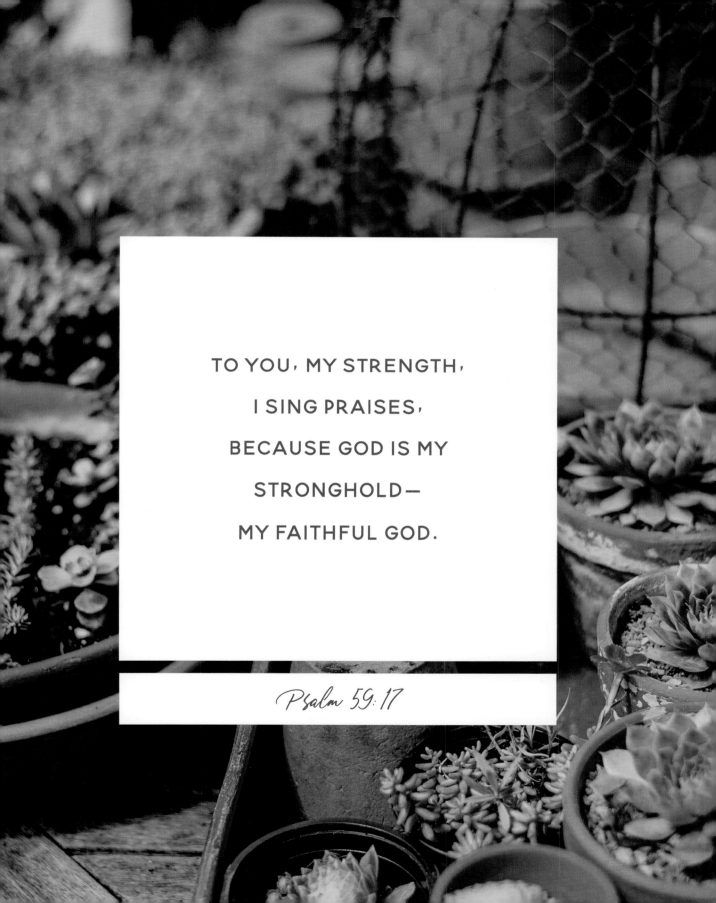

TO YOU, MY STRENGTH,

I SING PRAISES,

BECAUSE GOD IS MY

STRONGHOLD—

MY FAITHFUL GOD.

Psalm 59:17

WEEK SIX

Weekly Reflection ——————————————

Read Psalm 56-60

PARAPHRASE THE PASSAGE FROM THIS WEEK.

WHAT DID YOU OBSERVE FROM THIS WEEK'S TEXT
ABOUT GOD AND HIS CHARACTER?

WHAT DOES THE PASSAGE TEACH ABOUT THE CONDITION OF MANKIND
AND ABOUT YOURSELF?

HOW DOES THIS PASSAGE POINT TO THE GOSPEL?

HOW SHOULD YOU RESPOND TO THIS PASSAGE?
WHAT IS THE PERSONAL APPLICATION?

WHAT SPECIFIC ACTION STEPS CAN YOU TAKE
THIS WEEK TO APPLY THE PASSAGE?

What is the gospel?

Thank you for reading and enjoying this study with us! We are abundantly grateful for the Word of God, the instruction we glean from it, and the ever-growing understanding about God's character from it. We're also thankful that Scripture continually points to one thing in innumerable ways: The Gospel.

We remember our brokenness when we read about the Fall of Adam and Eve in the garden of Eden (Genesis 3), when sin entered into a perfect world and maimed it. We remember the necessity that something innocent must die to pay for our sin when we read about the atoning sacrifices in the Old Testament. We read that we have all sinned and fallen short of the glory of God (Romans 3:23), and that the penalty for our brokenness, the wages of our sin, is death (Romans 6:23). We all are in need of grace, mercy, and most importantly: we all need a Savior.

We consider the goodness of God when we realize that He did not plan to leave us in this dire state. We see His promise to buy us back from the clutches of sin and death in Genesis 3:15. And we see that promise accomplished with Jesus Christ on the cross. Jesus Christ knew no sin yet became sin so that we might become righteous through His sacrifice (2 Corinthians 5:21.) Jesus was tempted in every way that we are and lived sinlessly. He was reviled, yet still yielded Himself for our sake, that we may have life abundant in Him. Jesus lived the perfect life that we could not live, and died the death that we deserved.

The Gospel is profound yet simple. There are many mysteries in it that we can never exhaust this side of Heaven, but there is still overwhelming weight to its implications in this life. The Gospel is the telling of our sinfulness and God's goodness, and this gracious gift compels a response. We are saved by grace through faith, (Ephesians 2:9) which means that we rest with faith in the grace that Jesus Christ displayed on the cross. We cannot save ourselves from our brokenness or do any amount of good works to merit God's favor, but we can have faith that what Jesus accomplished in His death, burial, and resurrection was more than enough for our salvation and our eternal delight. When we accept God, we are commanded to die to our self and our sinful desires, and live a life worthy of the calling we've received (Ephesians 4:1). The Gospel compels us to be sanctified, and in so doing, we are conformed to the likeness of Christ Himself.

This is hope. This is redemption. This is the Gospel.

He made the one who did not
know sin to be sin for us,
so that in him we might become
the righteousness of God.

2 CORINTHIANS 5:21

FOR STUDYING GOD'S
WORD WITH US!

CONNECT WITH US:

@THEDAILYGRACECO

@KRISTINSCHMUCKER

CONTACT US:

INFO@THEDAILYGRACECO.COM

SHARE:

#THEDAILYGRACECO

#LAMPANDLIGHT

WEBSITE:

WWW.THEDAILYGRACECO.COM